Michael Carter-Williams: The Inspiring Story of One of Basketball's Young Elite Point Guards

An Unauthorized Biography

By: Clayton Geoffreys

Table of Contents

Foreword

When NBA draft experts projected the 2013 NBA Draft, no one would have expected or anticipated that Michael Carter-Williams (MCW) would end the year as the Rookie of the Year. Michael Carter-Williams did just that. Starting out in full swing when the regular season began, MCW quickly became the hottest thing to arrive in Philadelphia since Allen Iverson. MCW's remarkable rookie season is one for the record books as he reignited a city and a rebuilding franchise with hope for the future. Winning 104 of the 124 possible first-place votes, Michael Carter-Williams easily emerged as the hottest new addition to the NBA. However, he did not make it to the big stage by accident—it was through hard work and perseverance that MCW was able to make it to the NBA. Thank you for downloading *Michael Carter-Williams: The Inspiring Story of One of Basketball's Young Elite Point Guards.* In this unauthorized biography, we will learn MCW's incredible life story and impact on the game of basketball. Hope you enjoy and if you do, please do not forget to leave a review! Also, check out my website at claytongeoffreys.com to join my exclusive list where I let you know about my latest books and give you goodies!

Cheers,

Clayton Geoffreys

Visit me at www.claytongeoffreys.com

Introduction

The 2013 NBA Draft was not supposed to have any budding stars. Player personnel experts could not agree upon a clear consensus No. 1 pick among the crop of entrants. The media panned the draft for its lack of star quality, dogging the Cleveland Cavaliers for selecting UNLV power forward Anthony Bennett with the top pick. There was not supposed to be a special star in that year's lottery, and finding talent outside the top 10 was not even a conversation. Teams were rumored to be setting themselves up for a lottery pick in the upcoming 2014 Draft, which featured 'can't-miss' players such as Andrew Wiggins of Kansas and Jabari Parker of Duke.

But there was one name that defied expectations. One player rose up to challenge the thought that none of the rookies could make an immediate impact that season. Apparently, Philadelphia 76ers point guard Michael Carter-Williams (MCW) did not receive the memo.

MCW came into the NBA as an unconventional rookie. Standing at 6'6" and with arms that could stretch out to forever, Carter-Williams was a point guard in the mold of the likes of Penny Hardaway, Magic Johnson, and Jason Kidd. He was tall, long, and athletic. But he was never highly-touted, especially since his draft class was not all that unusual, either.

But Carter-Williams proved the world wrong by doing exactly what people thought he would not do—excel. In the rookie's first game as the starting point guard for a rebuilding Philadelphia 76ers team, he outshone even LeBron James himself to lead his squad past the powerhouse Miami Heat. With 22 points, seven rebounds, 12 assists, and nine steals, Carter-Williams immediately showed the NBA what he could do at his peak.

With a steady performance the entire season, Carter-Williams was eventually named the NBA's 2013 Rookie of the Year by receiving 104 out of a possible

124 first-place votes after becoming just the third player since 1950-51 (Oscar Robertson in 1960-61 and Alvan Adams in 1975-76) to lead all rookies in scoring, rebounding and assists. Carter-Williams averaged 16.7 points, 6.3 assists, 6.2 rebounds and 1.86 assists during his rookie campaign.

His stats also stood up well when compared to veteran players, placing him sixth overall in the league in steals and tied for 11th in assists. Carter-Williams proved that his draft class did have a star pupil as he joined past NBA valedictorians Oscar Robertson and Magic Johnson as the only players to average at least 16 points, six rebounds, and six assists as a rookie. Not bad company to be with.

Carter-Williams also led all rookies in player efficiency rating. He had a much better value added than the rest of the rookie class. However, like many NBA rookies, he had his struggles. Being the lone bright spot in an otherwise disappointing Philadelphia

76ers season, Williams had to carry the load by himself. He would often struggle from the field, and his shooting remained his biggest chink.

But nevertheless, Michael Carter-Williams did what he could to make an impact in just his first season in the NBA. His team may have had an awful showing the entire year, but he never gave up from start to finish. Just looking at him, one would say that MCW would become the point guard of the future of the 76ers. Unfortunately, that would not be the case.

But while MCW's rookie season was one where he defied expectations and exceeded what scouts and analysts thought of him, it would turn out that his come-out party that season would be his finest yet. He would come out of his rookie season looking to take the league by storm. However, the Philadelphia 76ers had other plans.

Putting up terrific all-around numbers across the board for Philly in his second season, there was not questioning that Carter-Williams was the best player on the roster. Nevertheless, the Philadelphia 76ers wanted him out, hoping they could land a higher spot in the succeeding NBA Drafts. Michael Carter-Williams was so good that he was starting to make the lowly 76ers look competitive. But it was his abilities that had him getting shipped over to the Milwaukee Bucks to start anew as that team's point guard of the future.

While it was a controversial move on the part of Philly to transfer a bright young talent like Michael Carter-Williams, who just won the Rookie of the Year, to tank for the next draft classes, the long and versatile point guard was still willing to start fresh with a new franchise. The Bucks that season were trying to compete for a playoff spot and their young and long roster was fit for an equally young and long point guard such as MCW. Best of all, he was joining head coach Jason Kidd, who played a similar brand of basketball in his heydays as Carter-Williams did.

With Michael Carter-Williams leading the way and becoming one of the integral parts of an upcoming young and talented team such as the Milwaukee Bucks, the NBA should be put on notice with what that team could do. On his part, MCW was out to prove that his rookie season was not a fluke and that he could surely become one of the best young point guards the NBA could ever have in his era.

Chapter 1: Childhood and Early Life

Carter-Williams was born into an athletic family on October 10, 1991, in Hamilton, Massachusetts to Mandy Carter and Earl Williams. Carter and Williams met while attending Salem State University (then known as Salem State College) in Salem, Massachusetts as student athletes. Both Mandy and Earl were playing college basketball at the time.[i]

Michael Carter-Williams was named after his grandfather Michael Carter. The grandfather was once named Leroy, but due to racial discrimination in those times, Leroy had to go by the name Mike because it sounded whiter than his real name. Carter worked mainly as a manual laborer for the majority of his younger days. Because he worked his body to physical exhaustion all those years, he became physically challenged by the time his grandson was born. Luckily, MCW would inherit his hard work.[ii]

After the young Carter-Williams was born, Carter raised her son as a single mother, living in five apartments within five years. Carter's mom passed away nine months after the birth of Carter-Williams, causing the two to depend on one another on many levels, thus beginning the great mother and son bond that remains alive today.

While his parents never married and broke up when Carter-Williams was an infant, Carter married Zach Zegarowski when Carter-Williams was four years old. She was then known as Mandy Carter-Zegarowski. Zegarowski had played college basketball at the University of Massachusetts, Lowell, and also spent ten years as the boys' basketball coach at powerhouse Charlestown (Mass.) High School.

Carter-Williams grew up with a parenting team, as both his stepfather and biological dad played roles in his upbringing, in addition to the steadying force of his mother. Zegarowski used to work out with a young

Carter-Williams at Miles River Middle School in South Hamilton, Massachusetts before the family built its backyard court, pushing the nine-year-old to his physical limits.

Zegarowski, though not the biological father of Carter-Williams, was the one dictating how the future Rookie of the Year would develop his basketball skills. As a basketball coach in Charlestown in Boston, Zegarowski put his stepson through all the hard training that he would usually put his older players through. It would even get so tough at times that MCW would seem like he was in the mood to quit. There was only so much a nine-year-old boy could take.[ii]

The stepfather would spend most of his free time working on the basketball maturation of Michael Carter-Williams. It would even get to a time when he would pit the middle school boy against bigger, older, and more athletic high school kids playing in the AAU. That was how hard the basketball training MCW was getting from his stepfather.[ii] But he and Zegarowski did it for the betterment of his future basketball career.

Despite the distance from his son, Earl Williams never tried to back out of his fatherly duties to MCW. Earl would take local transportation all the way from Cambridge just to see his son from time to time. Williams would tend to the psychological aspects of his child's maturation. Carter-Williams' dad would help his son to remain calm and not be frustrated from competing against older and physically stronger boys. Using another strategy, Williams would never allow his son to seek autographs from NBA players in hopes of preventing his son from ever being in awe of another basketball player. [ii]

Williams was there to be the psychological counselor of his developing child. He knew how tough the training regimen that Michael Carter-Williams was going through, but he recognized and thanked

Zegarowski for instilling into his son the values of working hard on basketball skills.

Though Williams was an assistant basketball coach himself, he chose the role of being a father rather than being MCW's coach. As Carter-Williams would say, Earl was the force that kept him going and kept him believing in himself. Earl Williams had his son motivated into staying stable through whatever hardships the young guard would face in his life.

But no family would ever be complete without a mother. Mandy Carter-Zegarowski played the role of a caregiver to her son, who was always pushing himself harder and harder every day.[ii] Mandy was always on the sidelines ready to cheer and take care of her son no matter what. Even to this day, she is still a guiding force in MCW's life as she is the young player's manager.

Chapter 2: High School Years

Following in his family's footsteps, Carter-Williams played ball while at Hamilton-Wenham Regional High School in Hamilton, Massachusetts. Though he was just 5-foot-9 as a freshman, Carter-Williams led his team and conference in scoring with 20 points per game while sinking 52-percent of his 3-point attempts en route to the league championship game.

He transferred to St. Andrew's School in Barrington, Rhode Island – a non-denominational boarding school of 213 students – for his final three years of high school, where he lived in a dormitory. It was a time in his life that instilled discipline in the young man. The school featured a strict schedule of schooling, practices, and workouts, waking up by 7 a.m. and turning lights out by 11 p.m. Being away at school helped mature the promising young player, who also played quarterback for the football squad and sat behind the plate for the baseball team.

After the transfer, it was in his sophomore year when he realized his potential as a future basketball star. Mike Hart, one of his high school coaches at St. Andrew's, was a witness to the young kid's metamorphosis into a budding star. He also saw how MCW hit the growth spurt that made him into a matchup nightmare at the point guard spot. After seeing Carter-Williams' real and figurative growth, Hart knew that the young point guard would someday dominate the college scene and get drafted in the NBA.[iii]

The former 5'9" guard, when he was brought in to play for St. Andrew's, did not resemble the player he is today. He was short and did not have the skills that most guards have. But he developed slowly into a player that, as Hart said, resembled Shaun Livingston. Both players played the point guard position standing taller than most of their matchups.

Even Leo Papile, MCW's AAU coach, believed that the kid had what it took to be great. He knew that what made Carter-Williams unusual for his position was his height and length. Even though he stood taller than most of his opponents, the point guard mentality never disappeared. MCW would dominate in pick and roll situations under Papile's system. His growth spurt might have even affected his maturity because Carter-Williams already had the leadership skills and mentality of a player beyond his age.[iii]

It was not until the end of his sophomore season that his family started to get looks at Division I schools and attention from head coaches. In October 2009, after averaging just more than 13 points per game as a sophomore for St. Andrew's, Carter-Williams decided to commit verbally to Syracuse. He had also received scholarship offers from Providence, Virginia Tech, Florida State, Virginia, Notre Dame, and Clemson, among others, but felt most comfortable on the upstate New York campus. Graduating from St. Andrew's in

2011, he became the first player from a Rhode Island high school to be named a McDonald's All-American.

As his basketball stock began to rise, attention from colleges increased as he went on to score 2,260 career points at St. Andrews. He averaged 27 points, eight rebounds, and seven assists as a senior. Carter-Williams also showcased his intangibles at St. Andrews, making the honor roll (3.2 grade-point average) for his final two years of high school and performing in the school's musical performance of Aladdin.

His scholarly ways are still evident in his life today as Carter-Williams has shown an understanding of personal finances, having his salary deposited into a trust that he can not touch for three years. Instead of living off his NBA salary, everyday expenses come from money earned through his endorsement deals. It is a family affair for Carter-Williams when it comes to business decisions; the $4.5 million that he's due is off limits due in large part to the advice of his mother.

Despite becoming a common name in high school in his senior year, many doubted whether he could take his talents to the next level in college. Carter-Williams had a tendency of disappearing when the games got tough. It seemed that would have been the case in a match against a powerful DeMatha Catholic team. After ruining a dunk in the opening moments of the game, MCW and his team had their backs up against the wall throughout the entirety of the game.[iii]

MCW would suddenly show the killer instinct that many thought he did not have. He would lead St. Andrew's to a phenomenal 22-point fourth quarter to come back from a deficit and to win the game 49-46. He was technically a one-man show since he posted 26 of the team's 49 points. Carter-Williams also finished the game with all around numbers of 6 rebounds, three assists, and six steals.[iii]

At that moment, nobody doubted what MCW could do in big moments. It was already undoubted what he could bring to the team once he got to college and, hopefully, the NBA. Michael Carter-Williams was off to Syracuse University as a hot commodity and as a heralded freshman hoping to make an impact on his way to a future career in the NBA.

Chapter 3: College Years at Syracuse

Despite a decorated high school career and a top ranking among prep stars, Carter-Williams had a quiet freshman year with the Syracuse Orange, waiting in the wings behind the likes of Dion Waiters, who left school early for the NBA following the 2011-12 season and was the fourth player taken in the NBA Draft. Carter-Williams also had to wait his turn behind talented upperclassmen Scoop Jardine and Brandon Triche.

It was a silent season for what would become one of the brightest young stars in the NBA. Carter-Williams never had a lot of impact even off the bench in that year. In fact, MCW's best performing night was a 13-point outing against St. John's.[iv] He never had a night like that in his freshman year. He was kept playing behind established rotation players while patiently waiting for his number to be called night in and night out.

Carter-Williams failed to start a single game in his first year at Syracuse, averaging just 2.7 points and 2.1 assists per game while averaging just ten minutes of playing time. He played in only 26 games while he was on the sidelines watching his teammates without even having a chance to do much. The young kid whose high school coach Mike Hart once described as a player that could make an impact in both the collegiate and professional ranks could not even make so much as a single dent in his freshman year. After that season, it seemed like MCW was on his way to a mediocre college basketball career.

But Boeheim and his staff knew they had a unique talent in waiting who was wise beyond his years, one of the hardest workers in practice and a total team player. Boeheim told Carter-Williams' mother to change any plans she had for her son because Michael Carter-Williams would likely not be at Syracuse for more than two years.

While the belief was strong on the part of the coaching staff, it was even higher on the part of Michael Carter-Williams who made it a point to improve on a personal level during the offseason. Ever the hard worker, MCW refused to wallow on the sidelines watching other players get more playing time than he did. He was not content with just playing the role of a rotation guy.

Carter-Williams would spend time in the offseason getting in better shape. He would often lift weights while improving his nutrition to get a bigger, stronger body. Over the course of the summer, MCW packed a lot of muscle weight onto his once lean and skinny frame. Other than that, Michael Carter-Williams also worked on improving his jump shooting by doing shooting drills because that was one of the flaws in his offensive game. The extra hard work over the offseason would prove to be what helped MCW improve his game tenfold coming into his sophomore season.

As the 2012-13 season was coming, playing time in the Orange's backcourt cleared up in Carter-Williams' favor as a sophomore, allowing the 6'6" guard to use his size and playmaker vision to average 11.8 points, 7.4 assists, 4.9 rebounds and 2.8 steals per game. Those were tremendous jumps from his numbers in his freshman season after barely even getting the playing time fit for a player of his talents. In his first year as a starter, he handed out 292 assists operating in Syracuse's pick-and-roll-heavy system.

In the history of Syracuse men's basketball, only one player had ever had more assist in a season when Sherman Douglas tallied 326 assists as a senior in 1988-89. Carter-Williams posted 11 games with double-digit assist totals as a sophomore, including a season-high 16 dimes in a 108-56 victory vs. Monmouth in a season-low 26 minutes of playing time for MCW.

It also seemed like MCW was what the Syracuse Orange needed that season. Ever the unselfish playmaker that knew how to use his size and length to his advantage, Carter-Williams went on to lead Syracuse to a No. 4 seed and helped the Orange advance to the 2013 Final Four – the school's first appearance since Carmelo Anthony in 2003 and its fifth overall.

While Carter-Williams would best Michigan's Trey Burke in the 2013-14 NBA Rookie of the Year voting (the Utah guard placed third), the then-Wolverine's team won the battle of what was billed as a matchup of elite point guards. In fact, it was just the second time since assists became an official statistic in 1983-84 when two players who averaged at least 12 points and six assists per game for the season had met in the Final Four. The previous time also featured a pair of future NBAers when North Carolina and Raymond Felton met Illinois and Deron Williams in the 2005 National Championship. However, both players failed to meet individual expectations with Burke scoring just seven points on 1-of-8 shooting.

MCW also become one of the best defenders for the Syracuse Orange, especially because of his ability to reach long with his height and length. He could easily intercept passes from the top of the key while being a focal point of the Orange's zone defense. And with his size and athleticism, Carter-Williams immediately became one of the best rebounding guards in college.

Perhaps his biggest blemish in college was a strange episode in December of his sophomore year when Carter-Williams was caught shoplifting in a local Syracuse mall. According to reports, he went into a department store fitting room, placed a bathrobe and gloves into his backpack, and then left the store. A security guard caught him, however, and Carter-Williams paid a $500 fine, admitting his guilt in writing. He was not arrested, and no charges were pressed. The Orange were 8-0 and ranked No. 4 in the nation at the time of the incident, which appeared to have little impact on the team and Carter-Williams' stellar sophomore campaign. Though Carter-Williams ultimately heeded the NBA's call before completing a degree in his two years at Syracuse, he majored in communication and rhetorical studies in the school's College of Visual and Performing Arts.

Chapter 4: NBA Career

Getting Drafted

Michael Carter-Williams was a rare commodity coming into the 2013 NBA Draft. He stood 6'6" with an NBA-ready body while also boasting a 6'8" wingspan. While his size and length were not rare for a guard or forward, what made him unique was that he was a point guard.[v] He was neither a shooting guard nor a combo guard. MCW was a pure point guard in every sense of the word and the position.

Physically, there was no doubt that MCW was a gifted player at the point guard position, especially because of his size and length. Other than those aspects, Carter-Williams was also a naturally talented athlete that had the ability to run the floor well and jump out of the building with his 41" vertical leap.[v] From a physical standpoint, you had all that you needed in a matchup nightmare at the point guard position because MCW could bully smaller playmakers while also keeping up with them on the defensive end because of his speed and athleticism.

No matter who you asked or where you went, nobody was questioning Michael Carter-Williams' ability to run the point guard position. He was a pure a point guard as anyone could be. At 6'6", MCW had the handles that could put to shame even smaller point guards. Aside from that, he was good enough to break defenses because of his quick first step and ability to change his pace. And with his long strides, he attracts guards whenever he gets near the basket.[v]

MCW's ability to break defenses down is where it starts. As a point guard, he possesses the same unselfishness that great playmakers in the past had. Carter-Williams' tremendous court vision coupled with his skills in making easy tough passes was what brought him and the Syracuse Orange to the dance in his second season in college.[v]

Michael Carter-Williams, with his excellent passing skills and court vision, always had the ability to find open shooters out on the wings or corners after he breaks and attract defenses when he drives to the basket. With his height and length, it never seemed tough for him to make skip passes to wide open teammates or shoot his dimes through gaps and outstretched arms. With his skills at making plays, there was no wonder why MCW ranked third in assists in the entire nation during his sophomore season.[v]

Playmaking was not the only skill that Carter-Williams brought into the NBA Draft. Going back to his ability to break defenses, MCW could also score by himself instead of making passes to open teammates whenever he drove to the basket. He was always athletic and big enough to finish baskets at the rim while also possessing the tools needed to make acrobatic layups.

At the rebounding end, Michael Carter-Williams was arguably one of the better backcourt players in the

2013 class at collecting missed shots. Similar to all-around playmakers before him like Jason Kidd, Mark Jackson, and Magic Johnson, MCW knows how to use his size and athleticism to grab rebounds and start fastbreak opportunities from that point. It will not be a surprise if he ends up being one of the better rebounding point guards in the NBA when he finally matures.[v]

Defensively, Carter-Williams was never a slouch. At his size, he could defend multiple positions on the floor, especially because he had the length and athleticism needed to keep up with every perimeter guy. MCW was always smart enough to use his speed and long arms in intercepting passes to force turnovers. His quick hands also allowed him to make steals up front during one-on-one situations.[vi]

But there were certain aspects of his game that prevented Michael Carter-Williams from being the best in his draft class. Offensively, MCW was always limited. Aside from his occasional bursts of speed and athletic plays near the basket, there was not a lot that Carter-Williams could do. His perimeter shooting was always suspect. That was always his main weakness on the offensive end. No matter how hard he worked on his jumper, MCW always seemed to lack the proper mechanics and mindset needed of a capable shooter.[v]

In college, you would often see defenders sagging off Michael Carter-Williams, daring him to make plays instead of having him getting his teammates on a roll offensively. Those kinds of situations exposed Carter-Williams for the mediocre scorer that he was compared to the other guards of his draft class. MCW would often struggle to make shots when left open. Most of the time, he would even hesitate to shoot the ball at all because of his lack of confidence in his shot.[v]

And while Carter-Williams already possessed skills that could be utilized in the NBA especially because of his size, the problem that scouts saw was that there was no knowing how high of a ceiling he had. At the age of 22 coming into the NBA, MCW was not exactly the youngest guy in the draft class. His age alone put to question how much time he had to improve on his game.[vi]

Additionally, not a lot of people believed that Michael Carter-Williams had a lot of potential to grow. He might have already reached his peak form in his sophomore year in college when he broke out to become one of the best point guards in the amateur ranks. But nobody knows if he could still improve from that point. If you are a rebuilding team, you would not know if MCW had the qualities of a future star, or if he would just end up being a rotation guy during his career.[vi]

Despite the setbacks and weaknesses to his game, there was almost no doubting that Michael Carter-Williams was going to end up getting drafted in the first round and the lottery. He might have even had what it took to get drafted in the top 10 especially because of how weak his class was. But the sure thing was that he was going to make it to the big leagues no matter what.

Come draft day, Carter-Williams had to sit through ten selections (including the sixth overall pick when the New Orleans Pelicans drafted Nerlens Noel from Kentucky, then trading Noel's rights to Philadelphia in a draft-day deal) before the 76ers selected the Syracuse University product with the 11th overall pick. After getting chosen 11th overall, MCW was bound to become the lowly 76ers' starting point guard because of how young and weak the roster was.

Rookie Season

After being drafted 11th overall by the Philadelphia 76ers, Michael Carter-Williams was joining a young and inexperienced team looking to start anew. They had just traded away Jrue Holiday, who was once an All-Star point guard, in exchange for Nerlens Noel, who would never play a single minute during the 2013-14 season because of an offseason injury. Because of the Holiday trade and the injury to Noel, MCW became the starting point guard and the rookie that the Sixers could bank on.

Though MCW was going to be the starting point guard for the 76ers that season, nobody expected him to perform as well as he did. The prevailing thought was that Philadelphia would go to either swingman Evan Turner or versatile forward Thaddeus Young for scoring and leadership. Center Spencer Hawes was also a viable option. As young and inexperienced a team the Sixers were, they had good veteran options to go to instead of relying on a rookie. However, it would turn out that Carter-Williams was going to be their best player that season.

Carter-Williams made some NBA general managers look foolish during his rookie debut by posting a near triple-double performance of 22 points, 12 assists, nine steals, and seven rebounds in his first professional game. His nine steals set a record for most NBA steals in a debut and tied the record for most steals by a Sixer in a single match. It was one of the most remarkable rookie debuts in NBA and franchise history. Not since Allen Iverson did a rookie score that many points in his first game for the Philadelphia 76ers.

His impressive debut came against LeBron James and the two-time defending champion Miami Heat, prompting Hall-of-Fame guard Magic Johnson to gush about the rookie phenomenon on Twitter. His stellar debut set the tone for Eastern Conference Player of the Week honors as he joined former NBA MVP Shaquille O'Neal as the second rookie to achieve this accomplishment. Carter-Williams also won the league's Eastern Conference Rookie of the Month honors four out of the six months it was awarded (October/November, January, March, and April), so his Rookie of the Year honor was not a tremendous shock to those who had seen his NBA debut.

For an encore, Carter-Williams followed up his game vs. Miami's Big Three of James, Dwayne Wade, and Chris Bosh with two more consecutive wins against top point guards John Wall (Washington Wizards) and Derrick Rose (Chicago Bulls) to finish victorious his first three games in the NBA. Carter-Williams posted 26 points and ten assists in the win against Chicago on 10-for-22 shooting, putting to rest – for a brief moment – questions about the guard's jump shot.

Though his performance at the start of the season was impressive for a rookie that ten other NBA teams had passed on, it was Carter-Williams' ability to make everyone look good that was what made him a hot topic early that year. Shockingly, the Philadelphia 76ers won their first three games that season despite their apparent inexperience and youth. They would, nevertheless, falter as the season went on.

His early success gave head coach and fellow Sixers rookie Brett Brown the confidence to give the young guard significant playing time. Carter-Williams logged an average of 34.5 minutes per game, joining first-year contemporaries Victor Oladipo (Orlando Magic) and Burke (Utah Jazz) as the only rookies from 2013-14 to log more than 30 minutes per game. Not coincidentally, Oladipo and Burke finished second and third respectively in the Rookie of the Year voting (Brooklyn's Mason Plumlee and New York's Tim Hardaway, Jr. were the only other players to receive at least one first-place vote).

Carter-Williams embodied the proverbial 'diamond-in-the-rough' tag. He ultimately outperformed those taken before him in the draft, joining one-time New York Knicks point guard and former Golden State Warriors head coach Mark Jackson as the second player drafted 10th or lower to win the honor since Jackson was taken with the 18th pick in the 1987 NBA Draft. Carter-Williams also became the franchise's second Rookie of the Year Award winner, joining Allen Iverson (1996) in the 76ers record book.

Carter-Williams' strong start to the season quickly got him noticed around the league and earned the 76ers rookie guard a trip to the 2014 All-Star Weekend in New Orleans. He suited up for Team (Chris) Webber in the Rising Stars Game, where his squad was defeated by Team (Grant) Hill 142-136.

Perhaps typical of a rookie campaign – even a Rookie of the Year season – Carter-Williams suffered from inconsistent play throughout the year, despite his strong start. For every All-Star caliber performance, such as the 27-points, ten assists, and 12 rebounds in an early December home victory vs. the Magic, there was an early April loss to the Utah Jazz that saw Carter-Williams connect on just two of his 13 field goal attempts. But even in the loss to Utah, he dished out nine assists and pulled down seven boards, highlighting his strong playmaking ability and hustle while reminding everyone that a consistent jump shot is what a budding star needs most to build upon the strong start to his NBA career.

Despite some impressive scoring outputs, Carter-Williams looked hesitant to shoot at times throughout the season. Defenders would often play off of him, respecting his ability to drive and dish, but not showing the same respect for his shot. If defenders had to respect his shot, they would stick closer to him, affording him an increased opportunity to beat them off of the dribble and break down the defense.

The development of a pull-up jumper will be especially prudent in the pick-and-roll, where defenders have been going under screens for Carter-Williams, making it more difficult for him to make plays. If Carter-Williams improves on his pull-up, defenders will be forced to go over those screens, in turn opening up a plethora of possibilities on the offensive end. Carter-Williams is able to be extremely productive offensively without the aid of a consistent pull-up jump shot and adding a more reliable release will significantly expand his game and what he can do on the offensive end.

One thing that Carter-Williams showed that he already possesses is resilience. Following his triple-double vs. Orlando on December 3, 2013, in a game that saw him on the court for 47 minutes, the rookie missed the next seven games with a skin infection and swelling on one of his knees. He then dropped 15 points and ten assists in 35 minutes of play in a home win against the Brooklyn Nets.

As the best rookie in the NBA that season, there was only so much that one single freshman player could do for a team which lacked chemistry, talent, and experience. The Philadelphia 76ers were the worst team in the NBA, having finished with only 19 wins at the end of the regular season. For his part, Carter-Williams tried his best to keep the boat afloat by averaging 16.7 points, 6.2 rebounds, 6.3 assists, and 1.9 steals. No matter how you look at it, those numbers were worthy of an All-Star consideration. That was how good and impressive MCW was in his rookie year.

Stagnant With the Sixers, the Questionable Trade to Milwaukee

With the Philadelphia 76ers' season ending early, Michael Carter-Williams decided to undergo surgery to fix a shoulder injury that had plagued him throughout his rookie season. As he was recuperating from his surgery, MCW would miss most of his team's critical events during the offseason. He would even miss the season opener for the Philadelphia 76ers.

After missing the first seven games of the 2014-15 regular season, Michael Carter-Williams returned to full form on November 13, 2014, in a game against the Dallas Mavericks. However, it was a return he would have wanted to forget because his team was walloped by 53 points. Nonetheless, he finished with 19 points, eight rebounds, and five assists in his season debut, hoping to recreate the personal magic he had in his rookie season.

On November 29, Carter-Williams had his fourth career triple-double in a game against the Dallas Mavericks once again. He had 18 points, ten rebounds, and 16 assists in that game and continued to show that his rookie season was not a fluke. Unfortunately, his team was still the same old disappointing squad from the past season. They would lose that game and would open the season 0-17 before winning one in Minnesota. Carter-Williams had 20 points, nine rebounds, and nine assists in his team's first win that year.

As his second season went on, Michael Carter-Williams continued to put up incredible all-around numbers from the point guard position. He would have two more triple-doubles and several other games wherein he seemed like an All-Star gunning for superstardom. But in most, if not all, of those outings, the Sixers looked like a sorry excuse for a team.

The Philadelphia 76ers were off to one of the worst, if not the worst, seasons in NBA history. It did not even matter that Nerlens Noel was back from his rookie injury. Not even surprise performers like Tony Wroten, Robert Covington, or KJ McDaniels could save them from that disastrous season. Not even the stellar efforts of MCW in doing everything on the floor helped Philadelphia turn their hopes around. It was truly a disastrous one for the Sixers that year.

And while Michael Carter-Williams was recreating the magic he had in his rookie season, it could have been argued that he was not improved from his Rookie of the Year campaign. While he had slightly improved his ability to make plays for his teammates that season, MCW was still the same old player. He still shot horribly from the perimeter, and he could not drain shots from the three-point line. And with teams giving him more attention, his field goal shooting was even lower than his rookie season. With the way he was playing that year, critics might have been correct in saying that MCW might had already peaked.

Despite minimal improvements to his game in Carter-Williams' second season in the league, there was still no doubting his place as the team's best player. At the age of 23, he still had a long way to go concerning improving his game. With more work in the coming offseason, he had the makings of a future All-Star. If there was a player that the Sixers could build on for the future, it should have been Michael Carter-Williams.

Unfortunately, the Sixers' ownership and management had other things in mind for their franchise. On February 19, 2015, Michael Carter-Williams was the centerpiece of a shocking three-team trade that sent the young point guard over to Milwaukee in exchange for a first round pick.

What was surprising about the trade was that Carter-Williams was the Sixers' best player for two seasons, and yet he was immediately traded without even having a chance to break out into stardom. He was also their best trade asset, but all they got was a first-round pick that did not even assure a top-notch talent.

The main criticism about the deal was that the Philadelphia 76ers seemed as if they did not care about winning or even making their fanbase happy. It seemed like trading MCW away was merely a ploy to lose more games in the season and get the worst record in the league once again in the hopes of landing the top spot in the next NBA Draft, which featured the likes of Karl Anthony Towns, Kristaps Porzingis, and Jahlil Okafor. Nevertheless, the good thing about the trade was that it was a way for MCW to start fresh in a franchise that valued winning. He averaged 15 points, 6.2 rebounds, 7.4 assists, and 1.2 steals in 41 games in Philly.

Fresh Start in Milwaukee, Making the Playoffs

After trading away Brandon Knight in the deal that sent Michael Carter-Williams over to Milwaukee, the Bucks were set to start their promising rebuilding process on the reigning Rookie of the Year awardee. In his first game as a Buck, MCW tallied 7 points and eight rebounds against his old team, the Philadelphia 76ers, on February 25. In that win, he played only 17 minutes as he was still trying to accustom himself to the system of head coach Jason Kidd.

In Milwaukee, Carter-Williams was finally playing for an established system that was predicated on Kidd's solid defensive mantra. The Bucks that season valued defense above all. It was the perfect fit for a capable defender like MCW because the team relied a lot on their length to force turnovers and tough looks for opposing teams.

As a 6'6" point guard, Carter-Williams was bigger and longer than most, if not all, point guards in the league. Joining him in the backcourt was 6'7" Khris Middleton. At the forward spot, the Bucks had the 6'11" Greek Freak, Giannis Antetokounmpo. Rounding up the long lineup were big rim protectors

Zaza Pachulia and John Henson. Using their size and length, the Bucks were a great defensive team. It was a perfect place for a big point guard like MCW.

It would not take a lot of time for Michael Carter-Williams to adjust to a new team, new environment, and new coach. His breakout game as a Buck was on March 9 in a loss to the New Orleans Pelicans. He had 25 points and seven assists in that match. His best efforts for the team were both 30-point performances against the Cleveland Cavaliers and no less than the Philadelphia 76ers.

Though MCW played his usual capable all-around style of play, the Milwaukee Bucks were at an even point regarding their wins and losses. Despite the addition of Carter-Williams to the lineup, the team was still unable to get out of the middle ground in the Eastern Conference playoff picture. In fact, they had more losses after trading for Carter-Williams because of how late it was in the season to adjust the young point guard into their system.

Nevertheless, the Milwaukee Bucks made the playoffs as the sixth seed with an even record of 41-41. For his part, Michael Carter-Williams' stats saw a dip in Milwaukee because of the slow pace that the team enjoyed. He averaged 14.1 points, 4.0 rebounds, 5.6 assists, and 2.0 steals in 25 games for the Bucks. Overall, he averaged 14.6 points, 5.3 rebounds, 6.7 assists, and 1.7 steals including his stint with the Sixers that season. Judging from his numbers, it was not the breakout season that MCW was hoping for in his sophomore year in the NBA.

Though Carter-Williams saw a dip in his role and numbers when he moved to the Bucks, the positive thing he could take out of the trade was that he was on a playoff team. The Milwaukee Bucks would face the favored Chicago Bulls squad led by former MVP Derrick Rose at the point guard position. Matched up with an MVP and a multiple-time All-Star, MCW had his hands full in his first appearance in the postseason.

In his first playoff game, Carter-Williams seemed a little jittery since the pressure was on him to try and contain Rose. He would not contribute much on the offensive end while allowing his matchup to score 23 points on a good shooting clip. Despite being bigger and just as athletic, MCW's inexperience was what Rose capitalized on. Chicago would end up taking Game 1.

After a poor performance of 9 points in Game 1, Carter-Williams played a little better on both ends of the floor in Game 2. The developing former Rookie of the Year was slowly adjusting to the physicality and pressure of playing in the postseason. He finished with 12 points as he limited Derrick Rose to 15 points on 4 out of 14 shooting. Unfortunately, the Bucks would still fall in that bout.

Back home in Milwaukee, the Bucks would play with a little more effort on the offensive end as their crowd inspired them to play with a lot of energy. On his part, MCW was off to what would become his best playoff game yet. He was an important factor in forcing two overtime periods against a much more experienced Chicago Bulls team. However, he was still unable to contain Rose, who had 34 points to lead his team to a double-overtime win. Carter-Williams finished with 19 points and nine assists.

With elimination looming over their heads, the Milwaukee Bucks played like a desperate team as they were fighting for their lives against the Bulls, who were trying their best to make it a quick series. It would take until the final possession of the game to determine whether the Milwaukee Bucks would go fishing early or whether they would fight for at least one more day. It was backup point guard Jerryd Bayless, taking over for the struggling Carter-Williams, who would make a game-winning layup to give the Bucks a win in that series.

Intent on not letting his backup take the majority of the playing time at the point guard position, Michael Carter-Williams would pull off his heroics in what is his best postseason performance. The former Rookie of the Year would attack the basket without any fear while making sure the rest of his teammates were contributing as well. On defense, he frustrated Rose using his length and speed. He would limit the former MVP to 13 points on 5 out of 20 shooting while putting up 22 points, eight rebounds, and nine assists of his own to win that game by six points.

With Game 6 played in Milwaukee, the Bucks had all the opportunity in the world to force an improbable Game 7 after falling 0-3 early in the series. What was supposed to be an inspired effort turned into one of the most lopsided games in NBA playoff history. None of the Bucks could score. On the other hand, the Bulls were rolling to eliminate Milwaukee by 54 in that demolition job.

After being embarrassed by the Chicago Bulls on his team's home floor, Michael Carter-Williams' first appearance in the playoffs ended in a way that was not to his liking. But it was a good start for Carter-Williams as he continues to grow with his young teammates in Milwaukee. He averaged 12.2 points, 4.5 rebounds, 4.8 assists, and 1.2 steals in the six games he played in the 2015 NBA playoffs.

Injury-Plagued Season, Decreased Role

While his second season in the league was more or less the same as his rookie year, Michael Carter-Williams' third season in the league was going to be less spectacular than the last two. Injuries, different styles, and several other factors contributed to what was another stagnant season for the former Rookie of the Year.

Offensively, the Bucks did not need a lot of scoring from MCW considering that they had improved on that part of the court. They had just acquired another long center by the name of Greg Monroe, who had proven himself to be one of the better low-post scorers in the league. Young wingmen like Middleton and Antetokounmpo were also going to improve drastically in scoring. Finally, the return of Jabari Parker from a season-ending injury in his rookie year was going to be an added punch to the Bucks, who performed poorly on offense in the past season.

Because of the additional scoring punch to the lineup, the Bucks would not rely on Carter-Williams for scoring as much as they had the last season, or as much as the Philadelphia 76ers did in his rookie season. What they needed from their point guard was his ability to make plays and his all-around skills on both ends of the court.

MCW would focus on making plays and on defense at the early juncture of the 2015-16 season. His ability to find open teammates and defend opposing guards were all evident at the start of the year for the Bucks. But his strong start would be derailed by an ankle injury that kept him out of the lineup for five days.

Though Carter-Williams was able to make a successful return on November 14, 2015, his next few games were mired by inconsistent plays on all aspects of basketball. Though his scoring was never really needed, no coach would ever want his players going through a rough shooting stretch over a course of a handful of games. Because of that, MCW's minutes were slowly dwindling down until head coach Jason Kidd opted to start Bayless instead.

Though he was benched for Jerryd Bayless, Carter-Williams played the same amount of minutes he did as a starter. Kidd chose to make him the all-around punch needed from his bench. At first, it seemed like a good idea to bench the former Rookie of the Year considering that he put up 20 points and five assists in 28 minutes when they won against New York on December 5. MCW even had 20 points and 11 assists off the bench playing against Chris Paul and the Clippers.

But while Michael Carter-Williams was still thriving in his role as a sixth man, Jason Kidd would realize that he needed the point guard back in the starting squad. After regaining his starting position in the middle of December, MCW would go on a four-game personal tear. In four games against the Clippers, Warriors, Suns, and the Sixers since regaining his starting spot, Carter-Williams averaged 19.75 points, 6.25 rebounds, and six assists. What was even more impressive was that he shot over 51% from the floor in that stretch.

Carter-Williams, though still inconsistent at times, was beginning to develop slowly into a capable scorer and a regular all-around presence for the Milwaukee Bucks as the season went on. But while MCW was playing well, the Bucks were not. They were far off from the defensive pace that got them a spot as the sixth seed in the playoffs in the past season. For some odd reason, the Milwaukee Bucks, who were supposed to be better than they were a year ago, could not get over the hump.

What made things worse for Milwaukee was when Michael Carter-Williams, their best point guard, suffered a torn labrum in his left hip early in February. The injury would keep him out of the lineup for the rest of the season, and that spelled doom for an already struggling Bucks team. In 54 games that season, MCW averaged 11.5 points, 5.1 rebounds, 5.2 assists, and 1.5 steals. His field goal shooting dramatically improved from 39.6% to 45.2%.

While Michael Carter-Williams is expected to make a full recovery in time for the 2016-17 season, many now question his place on the Milwaukee Bucks squad especially with how Jason Kidd began to start Giannis Antetokounmpo at the point guard position in MCW's absence. With the 6'11" Greek Freak starting as the playmaker for the Bucks, the Bucks might even reconsider MCW as an expendable piece if he fails to recreate the magic he had in his rookie season.

Chapter 5: Carter-Williams' Personal Life

It has been a real family affair to this point in Carter-Williams' NBA career with his mom handling much of the everyday management duties associated with being a budding professional basketball star. The 2013-14 NBA Rookie of the Year is quick to credit his mom, who serves as his manager, for his success. Carter-Zegarowski, a 42-year-old mother of four, tends to her son's life, both on and off the court. She recently ended a 10-year run as head coach of the girls' basketball team at Ipswich (Mass.) High School to focus her attention on her son's career. That has helped Carter-Williams stay focused and allowed him to keep improving his game and not to dwell on Philadelphia's struggles as a young team and the epic losing streaks the team experienced (the 76ers tied an NBA record with 26 consecutive losses, matching the 2010-11 Cleveland Cavaliers for futility). Carter-Zegarowski has been known to try to correct her son's shooting form and voice her displeasure towards referees. She also traveled with her son to Orlando before the season for his first NBA summer league, with their journey being one of six stories documented in a two-hour special that aired on CBS.

Meanwhile, his stepfather, who lives with Carter-Williams, provides feedback on his games and practices. His birth father also continues to play a role in his life. The former college basketball at Salem State from 1988 to 1990 came from the same system as former NBA players Patrick Ewing and Rumeal Robinson. Carter-Williams was also a part of that system, participating in clinics run by former St. John's head coach Mike Jarvis.

With his family's support, Carter-Williams is quickly learning that his playmaking abilities can extend outside the court.

MCW has been making community assists within his adopted hometown of Philadelphia. Following in the footsteps of his educator parents, Carter-Williams joined forces with Mealey's Furniture in promoting reading and education for local youth. As part of the "Mad About Reading" program, kids were encouraged by Carter-Williams to read up to five books throughout the month of March. The point guard wants kids to know about the importance of exercising our minds and doing well in school and learning to feel good about one's self. That idea of having a positive self-worth has also shown in some of his other community and charitable endeavors, such as putting an end to the use of the R-word for someone with Down syndrome and also supporting Special Olympics in the greater Philadelphia region.

While at All-Star Weekend in New Orleans in February, Carter-Williams put more than his basketball abilities on display. He joined forces with other NBA players at a New Orleans school to help build a playground, and he had the privilege of presenting the Community Service Award to NBA Hall-of-Famer Karl Malone at the NBA Legends Brunch.

Ever the playmaker, Carter-Williams often takes to social media to seek an assist from his fans in helping those in need. While some athletes may fill their Facebook pages with images of their high-end sports cars or lavish parties, a look at Carter-Williams' public profile features calls to action to assist those in need in the impoverished nation of Haiti, typhoon relief efforts in the Philippines, and support for those battling Fibrolamellar cancer.

Perhaps Carter-Williams was born with a giving heart. Maybe he was just raised by giving parents and stepparents. After all, Carter-Zegarowski and her husband also raised two of Zegarowski's former Charlestown players, James Rodrigues and Anderson Santana. The two are Carter-Williams' best friends and help take care of Carter-Zegarowski's twins when she's in Philadelphia.

However, he also has first-hand knowledge of what it is like to face a family emergency and to find one's self in need of the community's support.

On March 23, 2013, the Orange were facing the University of California in an NCAA Tournament game in San Jose that would see the team advance to the Sweet 16. As Carter-Williams and his teammates were in the process of making their Final Four run that season, a fire started in the chimney of the Boston-area home where Carter-Williams grew up. News of the event was kept from Carter-Williams as he led the Orange to a 66-60 victory, but he could sense something was wrong every time he looked up into the stands and saw his mother. He was not told of the fire until after the game. His stepfather and twin brothers were at the home watching the game on television at the time of the 3-alarm blaze that drew fire personnel from all around Boston's North Shore and reportedly took more than two hours to extinguish.

The following morning, his sister sent a Tweet stating that the family was okay and unharmed. It was reported that Carter-Williams' dad and brothers were able to save a few photo albums, one of Carter-Williams' 1,000-point basketballs, and a few trophies, but little else. Though the budding NBA star is now in a position to help others in need, at the time the family set up public bank accounts to handle donations used to purchase clothing, food, and other necessities as they were forced to rebuild their home life.

Chapter 6: Impact on Basketball

Since Michael Carter-Williams' career is still very early, it is hard to judge how much impact he has had on the game of basketball. The one thing for certain is that he was indeed a diamond in the rough that made several teams doubt their choices in the 2013 NBA Draft.

MCW had an immediate impact on a struggling Philadelphia 76ers team in his rookie season. Arguably, his ability to do everything on the floor at a high level was what made him the Sixers' best player that year. Because of how he took the NBA by surprise and how he outplayed every other rookie that season, it was not a shocker that Carter-Williams ended up hoisting the Rookie of the Year trophy at the conclusion of the season.

While Carter-Williams' rookie season was impressive, he still had many critics and naysayers doubting his ability to become a real star in the NBA. They point out the fact that there was no other player in the Sixers' lineup that could even contribute well that season. It was also argued that MCW's rookie season was merely a fluke because of how young and inexperienced his team was.

With Carter-Williams playing at the same level as he did in his rookie season come his second year in the NBA, it seemed as if his detractors were right in saying that everything was a fluke and that he had already peaked in his very first year in the league. Despite the fact that MCW was still putting up numbers worthy of All-Star consideration, doubts still loomed over his head because of his weak offense. The doubts and rough nights he had with Philly all concluded when he was shipped over to the Milwaukee Bucks in the middle of his second year in the league.

In Milwaukee, MCW was off to prove that he was not a one-hit wonder and that he still had the makings of what could become a star in the NBA. Playing for head coach Jason Kidd drastically improved his mentality as a point guard on both ends of the floor. Because of that, he was an integral part of a Milwaukee Bucks team that made the playoffs that season.

Despite facing injury and bench duties in his second season in Milwaukee during the 2015-16 NBA season, Michael Carter-Williams quickly bounced back to show signs that he could still rise to someday become an All-Star talent. But when he was finally starting to show his class as a young talent, his season was quickly derailed by an injury.

While it is too early in his career for us to know tell how much Michael Carter-Williams has impacted or affected the game of basketball, we could still take out a few points out from his journey in the NBA. For one, you can never be too young or inexperienced to have an immediate impact on the professional landscape. In his first year in the league, Michael Carter-Williams took the league by storm to become the Sixers' best player and eventually the best rookie in the NBA.

And while Carter-Williams could have been the Philadelphia 76ers' next franchise player following the steps of the likes of Allen Iverson, management obviously had other plans when they shipped their best player over to another team. Though MCW had to adjust to a new coach and system, the fact that he was still averaging more or less the same all-around numbers as he did in Philly showed us his resiliency and his maturity amidst the controversies and the stone hearts of the NBA front offices.

What we could take from MCW's move to the Milwaukee Bucks at such an early stage of his career is that one man's trash is indeed another man's treasure. Philadelphia did not want to build their future around Carter-Williams, but the Bucks were wholeheartedly ready to take the young point guard into their roster hoping he could help rebuild what could be one of the best young teams in the NBA. And with his natural physical gifts and skills, there is no doubting that he could seriously make more memorable moments in the league as his career progresses.

Chapter 7: Future

At 6'6" and with arms longer than the average guard, Michael Carter-Williams is a matchup nightmare at the point guard position. He rises over all other point guards in the league, and he could also physically bully and intimidate the smaller playmakers in the NBA because of his size and length.

But size is not the only aspect of the game that got him the Rookie of the Year award. MCW is also a pure point guard in every sense of the word. He sees how defenses react while also possessing the ability to break it down whenever he goes to the basket. Moreover, Carter-Williams has terrific court vision that helps him find open teammates on the break and set plays.

And while we know that his physical gifts were some of the main factors in his ability to defend at a high level, it is his natural smarts and IQ for the game of basketball that helps him break opposing offenses down, especially for the Milwaukee Bucks, who use their length to disrupt and pressure their opponents. With all that said and done, MCW is truly a remarkable all-around young talent that could have a bright future in the NBA.

In the annals of NBA history, big guards such as Oscar Robertson, Magic Johnson, Penny Hardaway, Jason Kidd, and Russell Westbrook have become some of the best all-around superstars the league has ever seen. Those players were able to use their superior size, strength, and basketball IQ to impose their will on the basketball world with ease. Given his size and smarts, Michael Carter-Williams has a chance to be mentioned amongst those players when his career is all said and done.

MCW already has the size, length, athleticism, and IQ needed to become an elite in the league. But what Carter-Williams lacks the most is consistency. He has never been consistent in his ability to put up points on the board ever since he was in college. The top reason for that is that he was never a great jump shooter.

Luckily for MCW, some of the other all-around greats were never great shooters. Magic did not hit his jumpers at a high level. But Johnson relied on his other skills to contribute for the Lakers on the offensive end. Kidd, who would later become a deadly outside shooter, started his NBA career without a jumper. Given that, there is no stopping Michael Carter-Williams from one day becoming a terrific perimeter marksman as long as he works hard on that aspect of his game.

If one day Carter-Williams suddenly becomes a reliable offensive threat at the point guard position, everything would start from there. Defenses would keep eyes on him, leaving other people open for MCW to find. Coaches would also start relying on him to make the right plays and to hit the clutch shots whenever needed.

But if he might one day improve drastically on his offense, Carter-Williams will never succeed in the league if he does not develop the competitive fire and killer instincts that his all-around predecessors have possessed. We always remember Magic Johnson for his memorable clutch performances in critical situations. We also remember Jason Kidd for the many competitive seasons he gave the NBA for nearly two decades. And today, Russell Westbrook dominates the league because of his ferocity. But we have never seen half of those aspects in MCW at this early stage of his career.

With all that said, Michael Carter-Williams has all the physical gifts, talents, and smarts to become an all-time great. However, he has to work on his offense and his intensity for the game of basketball to actually become elite. But knowing the kid's work ethic, we know that he is somewhere out there working on his game harder than ever before. When his game and mentality finally mature into what is needed of him to become a superstar, we might soon be mentioning Michael Carter-Williams together with the likes of Oscar Robertson, Magic Johnson, and Jason Kidd.

Final Word/About the Author

I was born and raised in Norwalk, Connecticut. Growing up, I could often be found spending many nights watching basketball, soccer, and football matches with my father in the family living room. I love sports and everything that sports can embody. I believe that sports are one of most genuine forms of competition, heart, and determination. I write my works to learn more about influential athletes in the hopes that from my writing, you the reader can walk away inspired to put in an equal if not greater amount of hard work and perseverance to pursue your goals. If you enjoyed *Michael Carter-Williams: The Inspiring Story of One of Basketball's Young Elite Point Guards,* please leave a review! Also, you can read more of my works on *J.J. Watt, Colin Kaepernick, Aaron Rodgers, Peyton Manning, Tom Brady, Russell Wilson, Michael Jordan, LeBron James, Kyrie Irving, Klay Thompson, Stephen Curry, Kevin Durant, Russell Westbrook, Anthony Davis, Chris Paul, Blake Griffin, Kobe*

Bryant, Joakim Noah, Scottie Pippen, Carmelo Anthony, Kevin Love, Grant Hill, Tracy McGrady, Vince Carter, Patrick Ewing, Karl Malone, Tony Parker, Allen Iverson, Hakeem Olajuwon, Reggie Miller, Michael Carter-Williams, John Wall, James Harden, Tim Duncan, Steve Nash, Kyle Lowry, Larry Bird, Jason Kidd, David Robinson, Manu Ginobili, Paul Pierce, Ray Allen, Dwyane Wade, Kawhi Leonard, Pete Maravich, Draymond Green, Dirk Nowitzki, Jimmy Butler, Marc Gasol, Pau Gasol, LaMarcus Aldridge, Derrick Rose, Paul George and Kevin Garnett in the Kindle Store. If you love basketball, check out my website at claytongeoffreys.com to join my exclusive list where I let you know about my latest books and give you lots of goodies.

Like what you read? Please leave a review!

I write because I love sharing the stories of influential people like Michael Carter-Williams with fantastic readers like you. My readers inspire me to write more so please do not hesitate to let me know what you thought by leaving a review! If you love books on life, basketball, or productivity, check out my website at claytongeoffreys.com to join my exclusive list where I let you know about my latest books. Aside from being the first to hear about my latest releases, you can also download a free copy of *33 Life Lessons: Success Principles, Career Advice & Habits of Successful People*. See you there!

Clayton

References

[i] Spain, Sarah. "Mom Drives Michael Carter-Williams". *ESPN*. 15 October 2014. Web

[ii] Pompey, Keith. "Family Affair: The Making of Michael Carter-Williams". *Philly Articles*. 2 December 2013. Web

[iii] Dougherty, Jesse. "Next Level: After Breakout Sophomore Season, Carter-Williams bound for NBA Draft Lottery". *The Daily Orange*. 30 April 2013. Web

[iv] "Michael Carter-Williams". *Syracuse University Athletics*. Web

[v] "Michael Carter-Williams". *Draft Express*. Web

[vi] "Michael Carter-Williams". *NBA Draft*. Web

Printed in Great Britain
by Amazon